C000275083

A Beginner's Guide - 1

A Beginner's Guide - 2

THE
THREE
PRINCIPLES

A BEGINNER'S GUIDE TO THE
HUMAN OPERATING SYSTEM

Contents

A Beginner's Guide - 7

Introduction To The Three Principles

Throughout history, we have tried to understand our thoughts, behaviour and the forces that shape our reality, create our experience and mould our entire human existence. At the heart of this journey stands a profound revelation by Sydney Banks: the 'Three Principles' of Universal Mind, Universal Thought and Universal Consciousness. This book explores how these Principles form our beliefs, values, experiences, actions and even our business strategies. So whether you're seeking personal clarity or business insights, they are the starting point.

From comparing the operating Principles of the mind to the way a computer functions, the mechanics of a car engine and even how we watch a film, to understanding how businesses can leverage these insights for optimal operation, this beginner's guide provides an introductory view. Read on to uncover the profound depth and practicality of the Principles and their potential to change both personal perspectives and professional paradigms.

A note of caution: These Principles are a description of how we experience life. We use words to convey their meaning, but your own thoughts and insights will give these words your own meaning. The Three Principles are DESCRIPTIVE, they are NOT PRESCRIPTIVE. You don't 'do' the Principles, they are already operating within you. A realisation of the power and implications of the process behind the human experience is the next step here and this introductory book aims to be one of the milestones on your journey.

Sydney Banks: A Visionary and His Insights

An insight is an intuitive understanding or realisation about the true nature of something, often arriving as moments of clarity. One insight can change everything. One such insight was experienced by a humble man named Sydney Banks (Syd), a Scottish welder with no formal background in psychology or philosophy. In the 1970s, Mr Banks underwent a transformative experience that led him to a deep understanding of human nature and the workings of the human mind.

This personal enlightenment was not rooted in rigorous academic study or an arduous spiritual journey, but came as a sudden realisation shifting his perception of all life in the universe in the blink of an eye.

Syd's insights can be described as both revolutionary and timeless. While he didn't introduce entirely new concepts to the world, (he often said: "This is not new"), he distilled the essence of human experience into three foundational Principles: Mind, Thought and Consciousness.

His teachings provide a simple, yet deeply impactful framework for understanding the human experience at its core. Essentially, he described what was already there in an accessible way for all to understand.

The Foundational Importance of the Three Principles

The significance of the Three Principles lies in their simplicity and universality. They are not just another theory or psychological model. Principles are scientific theorems or laws with a wide range of specific applications. They are fundamental truths that underlie all human experience. These Principles apply to everyone, no matter who you are, where you come from or what you are doing in life. They are universal.

Universal Mind represents the infinite intelligence and energy of all life - the source of creation. Just as a computer requires electricity to function and cars need fuel to run, humans need the energy and intelligence of Universal Mind (or Mind) to think, perceive and experience life. We are it! It is the very essence of life and it is the energy source that powers everything. As you read this, you are alive and experiencing Mind in action right now.

Universal Thought gives us our creative power of thought. Our thoughts shape our reality. They connect the formless, unlimited potential of creativity with the material world where ideas take shape. Although thoughts are temporary, the power of Thought is constant. It has always been here and always will.

Universal Consciousness enables us to be aware of our thoughts and our surroundings. It is the power through which we experience life. This Principle is pivotal in understanding that our reality is not just a direct reflection of the external world, but a construct of our thoughts in the moment. When we begin to understand how this works, we get to see that our perception may be illusionary, created by Mind, shaped by our thoughts, and brought to life through consciousness.

Recognising the importance of the Three Principles can radically shift our understanding of life. Instead of being at the mercy of external circumstances, we begin to see that our internal world of thought creates all our feelings, actions, performance and results. Our entire experience of life is thought created. This realisation, as Syd Banks emphasised, has profound implications for mental well-being, personal development, optimal performance and our overall understanding of humanity and the human experience.

In our understanding of the process happening at all

times within us, we get to see that our relationship with thought is key. **We can't choose our thoughts, but we can choose, although it doesn't always seem like it, how to react to them.**

We may also catch a glimpse of the fact that **this process is happening at all times, from the inside-out.**

Crucially, we might even realise that **behind the noise of this constant chatter of thought lies a deeper wisdom, our intuitiveness, which is always available to us.**

In the following pages, we will delve deeper into these Principles exploring their implications and their interplay in shaping our perceptions, decisions and reactions to the world around us, hopefully giving you a glimpse of what is possible with a deeper understanding. Through perceiving how the Three Principles are working to shape our experience of life at all times, we embark on a journey towards greater clarity, peace and insight into human nature and experience.

"All we are is peace, love and wisdom and the power to create the illusion that we are not."
— Jack Pransky

Syd's Enlightenment Experience

In 1973, Sydney Banks, a 9th-grade educated welder from Edinburgh in Scotland, had a profound insight which catapulted him from being an insecure, unhappy man into one of the world's leading theosophers and philosophers, lecturing to universities and professors, as well as professionals in the fields of psychology, social work, law enforcement, education and business around the globe.

The deep insights he experienced on that day gave him an understanding of the workings of the universe, our place in it and how we navigate our way through life.

The story goes something like this (kindly edited and approved by Judy Banks): According to Syd's own verbal accounts, he and his wife Barbara went to a relationship seminar held on Cortes Island in British Columbia, Canada - not without signing up and then cancelling several times through fear and insecurity! This particular seminar encouraged couples to let their feelings out and argue with one another openly.

The couple were unhappy with this process and Syd and Barb (as she was known) prepared to leave the seminar to journey back home.

Before they left however, Syd, who described himself as an insecure mess at the time, engaged in conversation with a psychologist who was also attending the seminar with his wife. As they talked, the psychologist asked Syd about his problems. Syd told the psychologist that he was really insecure and elaborated on all the ways he felt this.

The next day, Syd and Barb bumped into the same psychologist and his wife who said that what Syd had told him the previous evening was total nonsense and that Syd was not really insecure, he just thought he was.

What Syd heard the psychologist say at that moment was: 'There's no such thing as insecurity, it's all just thought.' All his insecurity was only his thinking! He said it was like a bomb going off in his head. He described it as being enlightening and totally unbelievable, so he asked the psychologist if he realised what he had just said. At this point, the psychologist became insecure and replied, "Of course I realised what I said, or I wouldn't have said it". But Syd saw that he could not have fully understood his own words, otherwise he would not have reacted with such insecurity. Syd had heard the words at a much deeper level than had been spoken to him.

In the following three days after he had this awakening experience, Syd began to see truth after truth about life and the way we navigate our way through it. He barely slept as these realisations came to him.

He went to his mother-in-law's house (with whom he did not get on) and overheard her and his wife complaining about how happy Syd had been in the past few days, which he found incredibly funny. He laughed so loudly that his mother-in-law overheard and confronted him to ask what was so funny.

Syd, worried that he had offended her, stood up to talk to her and as he did so, looked out of the window and saw what he described as buzzing white light – the transcendent light of knowledge dawning upon him. In that moment he realised the true nature of Universal Mind as the formless pre-existing energy of everything.

Syd came to see that there are three formless Principles of Mind, Thought and Consciousness which explain the whole range of human behaviour and feeling states. In Syd's words: "They create all human experience."

He defined the Three Principles in his books as follows:

Universal Mind is the energy and intelligence of all life, whether in form or formless. Universal Mind, or the impersonal mind, is constant and unchangeable. The personal mind is in a perpetual state of change.

Universal Thought is a divine gift, which serves us immediately after we are born. It is the creative agent we use to direct us through life. It is like the rudder of a ship steering us through life.

Universal Consciousness is the gift of awareness, it allows the recognition of form - form being an expression of Thought.

Syd turned to his wife and mother-in-law and said that what he had just learned meant that he would be speaking to universities, lecturing to doctors and writing books and that their whole lives were about to change.

This worried them greatly, because here was this ninth grade educated welder who couldn't even spell psychologist, let alone teach one, making these bold assertions about the future! But Syd saw it and it happened precisely the way he envisaged. He saw with clarity that he would be spreading the word about these Three Principles to the world for the rest of his life. He did just this and it is due to Syd (Mr. Sydney Banks 1931–2009) and the Principles that this book is now in your hands.

Syd's primary thought was, 'Who am I going to tell first'? He went to speak with the pastor on the island that he lived on in Canada, presuming he would pass it on to the bishop and the bishop would tell his superior and eventually it would get to the media. That way, Syd thought, humanity would soon be able to see the innocence and blindness of our own egos and we would all wake up to the 'truth'... and the whole world would take stock and heal from within.

What Syd did not reckon with is that we all interpret things through our own perspectives, and each individual needs to reach a state of acceptance regarding this new level of thinking.

Essentially, Syd was not telling anyone anything new, he was just talking to them about a level of understanding that we can all see for ourselves if we look deeply enough. It may even be simpler than we present in this book.

That's the story of Syd's unique experience and how he saw how Mind, Thought and Consciousness create our personal realities.

Now that you have some of the history, let's explore in more depth each of the Principles.

We also suggest that you listen to Syd's own words, in his own voice, describing this experience. The Experience DVD from the Long Beach Lectures is available from Lone Pine Publishing: www.lonepinepublishing.com

"What you're looking for is in the most hidden place...right under your nose." — Sydney Banks

Universal Mind: Infinite Intelligence

Universal Mind refers to the omnipotent and omnipresent intelligence, or energy, that is the foundation of all existence. Many theological, spiritual and philosophical teachings and, more recently, science, such as quantum mechanics, have pointed to a singular source of intelligence (a zero point energy field or a unified field of consciousness) that underpins all of creation. Biologists call it the life force.

What sets Syd's understanding apart is the simplicity and clarity with which he saw the connection between our spiritual nature and our psychological experience, making it accessible and relevant to our everyday lives.

Mind is present in every moment, providing the energy and intelligence for every thought, feeling, emotion and experience we have.

In workshops, some people like to refer to this

intelligence as the universe, God or the energy behind all things. It is a universal reality and a constant presence that we label depending upon our conditioning. You can call it whatever you like, but it's logical to admit that there is some sort of intelligence and order behind life. We don't have to live life - life lives through us.

Here are some examples:

* Approximately 3,200 stars are born and die every second in the visible universe, according to Cornell Astronomy. They are created when regions of dust and gas in the galaxy collapse due to gravity. It's an intricate system that ultimately has led to life here on planet earth. The carbon in our bodies comes from stars, so we are literally made of star-dust. We don't engineer this, it happens regardless.

* When a baby is born, it knows how to cry to get oxygen and how to suckle for milk. It doesn't have to learn it. This intelligence is already within its tiny body. It's innate. We are born with it and we are born from it.

* When you cut your finger, your body immediately

works to repair the damage. The body knows what to do as the red blood cells create collagen fibres that form the foundation for new tissue. The wound starts to fill in with this new granulation tissue and fresh skin begins to form. It's a remarkable process, one that requires no intellectual interaction or thought intervention from you. It is Mind in action.

How Universal Mind Represents the Energy and Intelligence of Life

Just as the sun provides the necessary energy for life on earth, Mind fuels our existence with this infinite intelligence. It is the driving force behind every heartbeat, the spark that animates every cell in our body. It powers our experience of life. Without this energy source, much like a computer without electricity, we would be devoid of thought, consciousness and life itself. It is the fundamental, forming Principle, and it's more than just a power source; it's an intelligent force.

This intelligence is evident in the intricate patterns of nature, the complexities of the human body and also the profound insights that arise within us. It is the 'innate wisdom' that guides the growth of a seed into a towering tree and provides the intuitive nudges that direct our personal journeys.

We don't have to make thought and consciousness happen. We are alive and from the moment we take our first breath, Thought and Consciousness give us our experience of life in every moment. Mind is the power source.

The Interconnection of All Things Through Universal Mind

Understanding Mind (to the extent that we are able) also brings a profound realisation of the interconnectedness of everything, as now proven scientifically. Just as waves are part of the vast ocean, we are each individual expressions of nature's intelligence. We are nature, that is our nature. This means that at our core, we are intimately connected to every living being, every star in the sky and every grain of sand.

Quantum science shows us this through the phenomenon of quantum entanglement.

This interconnectedness transcends our physical reality. On one level, this may suggest that our thoughts, feelings, emotions and actions ripple out into the universe influencing the whole of creation. This may also imply that we have access to collective wisdom and experiences of all existence, past, present and future - knowledge that many gurus, theologians and philosophers throughout the ages have asserted.

Recognising this interconnectedness can be transformative. It means that our potential is not limited to our personal experiences or individual capabilities. By aligning with Universal Mind (we already are, but we may not always realise it), we can access insights, wisdom and creative solutions far beyond our intellectual understanding.

Mind (or whatever you wish to call it) is not just a philosophical, scientific or spiritual concept. It's a fundamental truth about our existence, offering a richer understanding of our experience, who we are and our place in the grand tapestry of life.

As we journey deeper into this understanding, we uncover the vast potential that lies within each of us, waiting to be realised.

"There is one Universal Mind, common to all, and wherever you are, it is with you, always. There is no end or limitation, nor are there boundaries, to the human mind."
— Sydney Banks

Universal Thought:
The Creative Power

At the core of this understanding is Universal Thought - the limitless and never-ending force of creation from which every individual thought emanates.

Consider the immense breadth of the ocean with its countless waves, creatures and deep-sea mysteries. Now, envision Universal Thought similarly as a boundless ocean, but instead of water and life-forms, it contains the potential for an infinite assortment of thoughts, ideas, beliefs and insights.

This ceaseless fountain of creativity is not limited by the shores of time or the depths of space and stands as an everlasting wellspring of innovation. The power of Thought has always existed, while individual thoughts have only surfaced (as far as we are aware) since we evolved the cognitive ability to recognise and dive into this vast potential.

Anyone at any time may be just as likely to get the

thought: "What am I going to have for my supper tonight" or "E=MC squared" (this thought actually came to Einstein when he was ill in bed with the flu and not directly trying to solve the problem of general relativity). As Syd said: "You are only one thought away from an entirely new reality."

How Thoughts Shape Our Individual Realities

Every blink, every breath and every heartbeat of our lives is fundamentally influenced by thought. Thought is the architect of the very fabric of our reality. It influences our perceptions, determines our reactions and shapes our self-image.

Imagine a serene snow-clad mountain landscape. Two trekkers observing it might have contrasting experiences. For one, the landscape might evoke feelings of beauty, tranquillity and peace, while the other might be overwhelmed by thoughts of the cold, survival and the challenges ahead. Here, the external stimulus is the same, but their individual thoughts create their separate realities.

The transformative power of thought doesn't stop at mere perception. Our self-beliefs, capabilities and aspirations are all steered by the compass of thought. One restrictive, limiting thought can act as a barrier, whilst an empowering one can be the catalyst for monumental shifts.

The Link Between Universal Thought and Personal Thinking

Our daily stream of individual thoughts, that internal narrative which comments on, critiques and constructs everything, is what we term 'personal thinking'. Although these thoughts might seem intimate and individualistic, they stem from the same expansive realm of Universal Thought.

Consider the analogy of Universal Thought as an infinite ocean, teeming with life and potential. Personal thinking can be likened to the waves on the ocean's surface; they might seem separate, but they are born from the ocean itself.

Recognising this intricate connection is one path to liberation. It suggests that our present way of thinking, irrespective of how deep-rooted, is but a droplet in the vast ocean of potential thoughts. This realisation implies that we are never confined to a single narrative or viewpoint.

Armed with this knowledge, we are free to unearth fresh thinking, see beyond our pre-existing beliefs and even sculpt new personal stories, whilst recognising it can seem hard for some to overcome deeply conditioned thinking at times. We go upstream from thought to its source, realigning with Universal Mind and welcoming new insights.

New Thinking is Available at all Times

Universal Thought stands testament to the infinite creative potential that lies within each individual. By discerning the dance between Universal Thought and personal thinking, we open doors to a profound understanding of our intrinsic nature and the power we wield in shaping our own separate realities and our collective mentality. Embracing this understanding can be both an empowering and humbling journey, steering us toward a life of clarity, creativity and purpose.

"It's not WHAT you think that matters, but THAT you think..."
— Sydney Banks

Universal Consciousness: Our Window To Reality

The Role of Consciousness in Shaping Our Experience

Whilst Universal Mind lays the foundation with raw (formless) energy and intelligence for existence, it is through consciousness that we gain awareness of our thoughts, emotions and the surrounding world - the world of 'form'.

Imagine a cinema projector. The reel symbolises our thoughts, while the beam represents consciousness. Without the beam, the reel remains dormant and there is no image on the screen. Similarly, in the absence of consciousness, all our emotions and thoughts stemming from Universal Mind would remain hidden.

Syd Banks saw that our separate realities are not a mere result of external events but are a consequence of our interpretation of these events. This nuanced understanding paves the way for a transformative perspective on personal responsibility - our ability to respond - and the power to create our experience.

"Someone once said to me, 'Are you telling me that chair isn't real, that it's only thought?' I said, 'Of course the chair is real. But it comes to you via Thought." — Sydney Banks

How Consciousness Allows Us to Perceive and Interact with the World

Consciousness is the bridge that connects us to existence. Via consciousness, we not only observe our environment but also actively engage with and experience our reality. We are participants in life as well as observers of it. From the tactile sensation of a gentle breeze to the profound depths of introspection, consciousness is the alchemy that transforms physical stimuli into lived experiences.

Delve into a moment as simple as savouring a piece of fruit. The tangible properties of texture and composition interface with our sensory receptors. But the magic of consciousness translates this physical exchange into the sweetness or tanginess we experience. What's more, this experience changes once our level of awareness changes. We have all eaten fruit and thought nothing of it, or remember a time when we ate fruit and it was a wonderful experience. The fruit was the same but our experience of it changed as our consciousness changed.

In the absence of consciousness, the world in all its splendour would still exist, but our personal experience of it would vanish. Beyond sensory perceptions, consciousness permeates every facet of our existence. Every choice, every discourse, and every action is a testament to consciousness interfacing with thought to give us a reality from moment to moment.

The Different Dimensions of Consciousness

Universal Consciousness, whilst a singular thread of

awareness, manifests in varied shades and intensities. Throughout history, philosophers, scientists, and spiritual leaders have commented on different states of consciousness. Just like the fruit example above, there are varying levels of conscious awareness.

How our brains generate consciousness from neural activity and billions of nerve cells remains a mystery. We can be aware of our consciousness, experiencing thoughts, feelings, and perceptions, yet despite advances in neuroscience, we cannot functionally prove our consciousness to others.

Consciousness seems to have various dimensions, encompassing different states and levels of awareness. For instance, a drowsy or half-asleep person experiences reduced awareness compared to someone in a state of stimulated arousal who may have heightened awareness.

Low Awareness: Even when unaware of our surroundings, our brain processes vast amounts of information, sending and receiving signals. This might not be apparent to us, as in the case of a sleeping person instinctively pulling a blanket for warmth, as the brain responds to cold signals even in sleep.

In states of stress, upset, anger, anxiety, or worry, our awareness may become narrowed, limiting our openness to new information or ideas and temporarily reducing our capacity for insight or problem-solving.

This state, sometimes termed cognitive or emotional hijack, 'out of flow' or 'off track', still allows the brain to perform background tasks, though our awareness of these processes is lessened.

High Awareness: This involves being fully present and grounded in the moment. It includes focused attention, detailed observation, big-picture thinking, environmental surveying, awareness of others, and an internal dialogue of intuition, emotions and thoughts. High awareness typically occurs in states of peace, such as in nature, relaxing in a warm bath, or engaging in enjoyable activities or exercise. This state is often referred to as being 'in flow' or 'on-track'.

A comprehension of these two dimensions of conscious awareness and every level or state in between provides a panoramic view of the human experience. It hints at our untapped potential for perception, comprehension and evolution.

"Each individual person surveys life according to his or her personal level of consciousness." — Sydney Banks

We can't choose our level of consciousness, but we can be aware of it. This awareness can indicate to us important information about how, or who, we are being and can lead us to make better decisions. Via our feeling state, we become conscious of our own level of awareness, which in turn gives us more opportunity to maintain our bearings and to act wisely.

You may liken our feelings to the engine warning light in a car letting us know when to pull over and stop driving. It acts as an indicator.

In many respects, Universal Consciousness, although an essential part of the process of how we experience life, is also something of a red herring in this context.

People can get stuck talking about states and levels of consciousness, when there's nothing we can even do about our own state or level other than be aware of it (or not). It's an integral part of the Principles as without it we can not experience anything, but it is less important than realising that we are only ever one thought away from a completely new reality - and knowing this is **always** a possibility.

"Feelings provide our moment-to-moment experience of life. They tell us the extent to which our perceptions are distorted by our moods and thought systems."
— Dr. George Pransky

The Interplay Of The Three Principles: How They Shape Our Experience

Understanding the Interdependent Nature of the Principles

The Three Principles are not standalone pillars. They are an inextricably linked system that forms all human experience - we call it The Human Operating System.

Here's a quick recap:

* **Universal Mind** is the energy and intelligence of life, the source from which all things emerge - akin to the electricity that powers a computer. Without this Principle, there is no life, no existence, nothing.

* **Universal Thought** is the software, the programmes and applications that the computer runs; an endless force creating every thought, idea, belief and insight. It shapes and defines our individual and collective realities.

* **Universal Consciousness** is awareness, the beam and the monitor screen that displays the content. Without it, we may not perceive or understand our existence.

The beauty of the Three Principles lies in the symphony of the system. Mind provides the raw potential. Thought shapes this potential into being and Consciousness allows us to perceive and experience what is formed from it. None can function without the others, much like a computer cannot usefully run without electricity, a screen and software.

The Power of Personal Creation: Crafting Our Own Beliefs

Isn't it a wonder that on a planet populated with 8.1 billion individuals, each of us holds our own unique set of values and beliefs?

These beliefs, whilst guiding our every action, all originate from a similar process. We think, we internalise these thoughts and those that resonate deeply with us become our beliefs. This mechanism operates universally for everyone. Take the well-known tale of Father Christmas as an illustration. Most of us as children embraced the story wholeheartedly. Yet there came a time when this belief was replaced with a new understanding. In both instances, it was a thought – acknowledged and accepted – that shaped our belief.

But here's the revelation: this process of forming, accepting or discarding beliefs is ongoing. Our life's narrative is a compilation of stories we tell ourselves, consciously or unconsciously. We often come across individuals entrenched in self-limiting stories about their capabilities, finances or relationships, but these are merely made-up: an innocent misunderstanding conceived by our own minds and solidified by acceptance in the moment. The mind only works one way - from the inside-out: Mind, powering thought and brought to life by consciousness.

Your reaction to this very book will be influenced by your pre-existing beliefs – some of you might dismiss it, some might embrace it, while others might be intrigued. Which of these reactions is the 'correct' one? Each reaction is valid and is a testament to the stories we have told ourselves over time.

The key takeaway here is that we are not just passive recipients of life but active crafters of our own narratives. Recognising that we are the authors of our life story offers a tantalising glimpse of mental and emotional freedom. True liberation lies in the acknowledgment that we are the storytellers in the first place. We are the creators of our own experience. We are doing it ourselves.

"All feelings derive and become alive,
whether negative or positive,
from the power of Thought."
— Sydney Banks

Implications Of Understanding The Three Principles

Remember: these Principles are not prescriptive, they are descriptive. You don't 'do' anything with them, but you can realise their importance. Much like learning new information can change your beliefs (Father Christmas!). Here are some implications we have found from our own experiences. There may be many more and you may be on the journey to discovering new ones, this list is not exclusive by any means:

Understanding How Something Works: When we know how something truly operates (like understanding germ theory), it can make a life-saving difference to humanity. Understanding how something works also means you know how something does NOT work, which is just as useful. Just ask a millennial attempting to use an old rotary telephone! The same applies to how our thinking works, as it's involved in everything we do and in many of the errors humans make.

Utilising Understanding to Our Advantage: We

can work with this knowledge, not against it. For instance, washing hands before surgery, a result of understanding germ theory, has saved countless lives. Knowing how thought works is crucial to understanding our life experience.

Life Experience Is Internally Generated: Understanding that our experience of life is crafted within our mind highlights the immense power and responsibility we hold. Businesses, relationships and personal decisions are essentially reflections of our internal narratives, allowing us to question and reshape them as we see fit.

The Process is Inside-Out: The process of the energy of life creating thought and feeling is constant. It works from the inside-out and is present from birth to death, for everyone, at all times.

Thought Realisation: This is a term used when we wake up to the role our thinking plays in our lives. Thought 'recognition' is life-changing. We begin to see the role of thought in **everything** we do.

Seeing Separate Realities: We can observe how others use the same thought process but achieve different results. This understanding fosters innovation, teamwork and compassion and helps us recognise when we're misled by our own thinking. It's so much easier to be tolerant with someone when we understand and appreciate separate realities (that what they are thinking and seeing might be different from what we are thinking and seeing). The same applies to conscious awareness. We all feel differently from day to day and from moment to moment. By acknowledging this, in ourselves and in others, we can better appreciate the richness of diverse perspectives and cultivate more understanding and peace.

Impermanence of Thoughts and Feelings: Thoughts and feelings are ever-changing. They're transient, like the weather, and we can't get stuck in them if we allow the natural process to occur. Much like the clouds in the sky, a new thought will be along any second and we don't have to do anything to make this happen. The system is designed to benefit us–we are wired for life. We experience a mental reset when our thinking shifts and this transition can happen effortlessly.

Life's Neutrality and Our Thinking: Life events are neutral; it's our thinking **about them** which gives them meaning (for us). This perspective allows us not to take things personally, even if we don't condone certain behaviours. Recognising that our experiences stem from transient thoughts allows us to be okay with not always feeling okay, knowing that situations change and our thinking about them also changes. It only matters if or when we think it does… and even THIS is an illusion!

Correlation, Not Causation: We are always feeling our thinking, rather than life directly. There is a correlation between events and our thoughts about them, thought being the intermediary between circumstances and feelings. This can seem almost impossible at times, especially when feelings are strong; however, our thinking about circumstances does change with time, so it cannot be the circumstance causing the feeling... it has to be thought in the moment. This is a game-changer when we get to see it for ourselves, but we can easily forget and get fooled by the illusion of life as it happens so quickly. It's the ultimate slight of hand magic trick and we are the magician.

The Present Moment Contains Everything: The past exists only in thought and the future is undetermined. Life unfolds in the present moment, the only time when we can truly engage with it. Being anchored in the present connects us to boundless possibilities. This can revolutionise areas like brainstorming in businesses, where tapping into this potential can yield unconventional and innovative solutions. Time, as we perceive it, is a construct of thought (or a stubborn illusion according to Albert Einstein).

The Future and Fresh Thinking: Worrying about the future is unproductive since we can't predict it and the fresh, in the moment thinking that might arise to assist us coming from the infinite potential of Mind - something which can get covered up and hidden from us, but which we can never be separate from.

Innate Well-being: Beneath all reactive thinking,

anxieties and worry, lies our innate well-being. Much like the presence of the sun, our natural state of peace, security, calm, confidence, hope, wisdom, joy and love is always present, although sometimes it gets obscured by clouds of thinking. Much like the analogy of the ocean with our personal thoughts as the surface waves, however 'choppy' it is up top, just beneath the surface it remains calm. [Note: Innate well-being can also get covered up by positive thinking].

The Role of a Mentor or Coach: Anyone who is grounded in their innate health can help others foster their own insights by providing an environment where individuals discover their wisdom and potential. It should be highlighted again that this understanding is not prescriptive. Being an effective mentor or coach is therefore not about trying to 'fix' others. Recognising one's innate health can foster self-compassion, well-being and resilience. This can be transformative for mental health initiatives, ensuring individuals understand their own worth and true nature.

Nature's Intelligence: The life force that created us

also guides our life journey. Trusting this intelligence means trusting the process of life, reducing anxieties and fostering a sense of purpose and alignment. There is less to do, not more. There is a nature to life. We are nature: we are that natural intelligence and seeing our true essence for ourselves can be transformational.

Fluidity of Emotions: Emotions are like waves, constantly ebbing and flowing. Our minds have a natural ability to reset and refresh. This mechanism ensures that we remain open to fresh insights and perspectives, even in challenging times. Recognising their transient nature offers peace and solace, knowing that challenging emotions will pass, making way for new experiences.

"If the only thing people learned was not to be afraid of their experience, that alone would change the world."
— Sydney Banks

Implications For Mental Health, Well-being And Personal Development:

Redefining Mental Health: Traditional approaches often focus on managing symptoms. Understanding the Three Principles, however, highlights the innate health and resilience present in everyone. It shifts the focus from what's 'wrong' to tapping into the inherent well-being and wisdom within, allowing this intelligence to resurface.

A New Paradigm for Therapy: Therapists and counsellors integrating the Three Principles approach often report transformative results. Instead of dissecting the past, the emphasis is on understanding the present moment and the power of Mind, Thought and Consciousness in shaping our experiences. By pointing to the process through which mental well-being operates, it allows the client to observe the transitory and illusory nature of mental torment and realise one's own innate health and wisdom.

Empowerment and Personal Development:

Recognising the creative potential of Universal Thought playing out through Universal Consciousness and the constant, supportive presence of Universal Mind empowers individuals to allow the system to do the heavy lifting, instead of trying to 'fix it' themselves. Resilience, well-being and cessation of repetitive stuckness, habits and behaviour occurs naturally.

An understanding of the Three Principles highlights hope for personal transformation and offers a revolutionary approach to well-being and mental health. It also allows both clinical and non-clinical practitioners to fully understand neurodiversity **without** labels or judgement.

"Life is like any other contact sport. You may encounter hardships of one sort or another. Wise people find happiness not in the absence of such hardships, but in their ability to understand them when they occur."
– Sydney Banks

Implications For Business

The complex world of business is replete with frameworks, strategies and methodologies. Nonetheless, the most profound and transformative perspective often remains under-explored – understanding the Principles behind The Human Operating System.

Mind, Thought and Consciousness offers a paradigm shift in how businesses operate, make decisions and shape their cultures. Most businesses try to address the issues they are facing by changing their behaviour, but all behaviours are the result of the thoughts and feelings of the individual.

All thoughts and feelings stem from the same process: Mind, Thought and Consciousness working in unison. Going downstream to the symptoms/results and trying to fix this is far less effective than addressing the causes upstream.

1. Universal Mind: Tapping into Intuition

This universal life force, prevalent in all individuals, is a powerful intelligence that allows businesses to:

* Harness Intuitive Decision Making: Moving beyond data and traditional analytics, businesses can access a deeper reservoir of intuition, making agile decisions that are both informed and inspired.

* Foster Innovation: Recognising the infinite potential of Mind allows businesses to create space for imagination to run free, ensuring they stay ahead of the innovation curve in their respective domains.

"The intuitive mind is a sacred gift and the rational mind is a faithful servant. We have created a society that honors the servant and has forgotten the gift." – Albert Einstein

2. Universal Thought: Navigating our Ever-Changing Reality

The thoughts we hold create our perception of reality. Understanding this Principle can revolutionise several business facets:

* Expansive Strategic Planning: Adept strategies look beyond current scenarios, remaining receptive to evolving perceptions and innovative, fresh thinking.

* Resilience, Agility and Adaptability: Grasping the fleeting, inside-out nature of thoughts allows businesses to maintain a positive focus on solutions, rather than wallowing or getting stuck in problems or by restrictions.

* Empathetic Engagements: Realising that every stakeholder, be it client or colleague, perceives reality based on their thought patterns, promotes empathy, transformational leadership and enhanced customer relations and teamwork.

3. Universal Consciousness: Crafting Tailored Experiences

Our level of consciousness dictates our perception and experience. This Principle has significant repercussions for businesses:

* Employee Well-being: By prioritising mental clarity and an understanding of the process that delivers innate mental well-being, businesses can offer comprehensive wellness initiatives for employees and

reduce absenteeism and presenteeism.

* Resonant Marketing: Understanding the consumers' experience helps brands create messages that strike a chord, leading to more effective marketing campaigns and sales.

* Cultivating Synergistic Teams: Recognising the unique perceptions of each team member can utilise diversity and foster transparent and compassionate communication, boosting team collaboration.

4. Incorporating The Human Operating System into Organisational Culture:

* Evolving Transformational Leadership: Leaders attuned to these Principles can champion a culture defined by clarity, diversity, collaboration, communication, innovation, intuitive decision making and empathy, culminating in heightened organisational synergy, productivity and output.

* Conflict Resolution: Armed with the knowledge that conflicts stem from individual perceptions, businesses can cut down on internal politics and 'blame culture' and craft resolution strategies that are both effective and compassionate.

* Teams Become Self-Managing: Once team members see how the system operates, they can begin to trust their insights, allowing their own wisdom to show up, ending over reliance on others and/or micromanagement.

While the Three Principles may initially appear esoteric, they are highly practical and essentially define The Human Operating System that every individual operates from. This is universal, no exceptions. Realising the profound implications of this understanding can catalyse a transformative journey for businesses, leading them towards enhanced operations, purpose-driven initiatives and resilient frameworks. In this ever-evolving business landscape, such a perspective might just be the cutting edge modern businesses need to open up next level transformation.

"Any company's greatest untapped resource is the innate wisdom, health and capacity for insight in its people."
– Robin Charbit

Real-World Examples And Anecdotes Of The Three Principles In Action

The names have been changed to protect identities.

Facing the Storm: After a sudden job loss, David felt like his world was crumbling. His self-worth was deeply tied to his job title. But as days turned into weeks, he began to see that his feelings of inadequacy were transient thoughts. Embracing this realisation, he started to see opportunities instead of setbacks and embarked on a new career path with renewed vigour. Trusting that he would be okay, he remained open to all possibilities and was soon snapped up by a start-up looking for experience as well as a visionary approach.

A Change in View: Lisa always viewed her colleague, Mark, as arrogant. But one day, after a heartfelt conversation, she realised her perception was based on a single, past misinterpreted incident. Recognising the impermanence of her own thoughts, and becoming curious about her colleague, she saw Mark in a new light transforming their working relationship forever.

The Artist's Vision: In a quiet studio, Leah, a professional artist stared at a blank canvas. To many it was just an empty space, but to her it was a world of possibilities. She felt overwhelmed, thinking of the masterpiece she wanted to create. But then she realised it wasn't the canvas that was daunting, but her own thoughts about it. Taking a deep breath, she let go of her expectations and allowed her intuition to guide her brush. The result was a painting that reflected her true essence, not her fears.

Mr. Johnson's Approach: Faced with a challenging student, Mr. Johnson initially felt frustrated. But instead of reacting, he paused and realised his frustration was a product of his own pre-judgements brought to life through thought. Seeing potential instead of problems, he connected with the student and listened deeply without trying to fix him. This simple, deep listening, non-judgemental conversation transformed a disruptive student into a classroom leader.

Emma's New Dawn: Trapped in the shadows of depression, Emma felt there was no way out. But upon introspection after learning how her innate health was not absent, merely covered up and obscured, she realised her feelings were shaped by her transient thoughts. Embracing this new insight, she began to see her emotions as passing clouds, leading her towards a path of healing and self-discovery, as her wisdom emerged from behind the clouds (it was always there, just hidden).

The Storm and the Sailor: Maria, an experienced sailor, was at sea when a sudden storm approached. To some, the violent waves and roaring winds might have seemed like a terrifying ordeal. Yet Maria felt a sense of calm. Her thoughts, shaped by her experience and trust in her own skills, remained calm. Despite the tumultuous surroundings, her conscious experience of the storm was one of respect and awe, not fear. She remained present and connected and navigated the storm with ease and grace.

Introducing Sarah: In the heart of the bustling city, Sarah, a CEO of a thriving tech start-up, found herself trapped in an addictive cycle. Every morning, before the sun even hinted its arrival, she was glued to her phone, sifting through emails, convinced that her constant vigilance was the linchpin holding her company together. This was her reality, her definition of success. But beneath this veneer of achievement, a storm of thoughts raged, shaping her habits and, in turn, her life.

One evening, as Sarah sat in her luxurious office overlooking the city, she stumbled upon an article about the Three Principles of Mind, Thought and Consciousness.

It spoke of thoughts as the architects of reality. A simple idea, yet profound. She pondered, "Could my incessant need to check emails be rooted in a deeper thought?" The realisation was startling. It wasn't the external pressures of her business driving her habits; it was her internal programming: her own thoughts.

Sarah began to see patterns. Her need to micromanage, and her reluctance to delegate all seemed to stem from a singular thought: "If I don't oversee everything, it will go wrong." This thought, she realised, was her addiction. It gave her a false sense of control, a temporary high of validation, but at a steep cost: burnout, strained relationships and a constant undercurrent of anxiety. Armed with her new-found understanding of The Human Operating System, Sarah embarked on a transformative journey. She began to challenge her perceptions. Instead of being a prisoner of thoughts, she became their observer.

One day during a team meeting, instead of diving into her usual mode of oversight, she paused, took a deep breath and had a profound insight. She spoke it aloud, as it felt right… "I trust my team." This simple shift in thought transformed the meeting. Ideas flowed, collaborations sparked and Sarah felt a weight lift off her shoulders.

With each passing day, Sarah consciously engaged the thoughts that empowered her, which aligned with the success she truly desired. She still had negative thoughts but could see the futility of engaging with them as they had lost the power and influence they previously seemed to have. She began to harness the life energy that powered her Human Operating System and she learned how to channel it into constructive habits. Meetings became platforms for innovation, challenges became opportunities for growth and success took on a whole new, holistic definition.

Months later, Sarah stood in her office, the city awakening beneath her. Her phone lay on her desk, emails waiting, but she was no longer at their mercy as their captive. She had broken the loop, redefined success and in doing so, had unlocked a deeper, more authentic potential. She had discovered the true power of The Human Operating System, the power to witness how her reality was constantly being shaped from the inside-out.

In the vast tapestry of the business world, success may not just be about profits or accolades. It's about understanding our internal programming, recognising the profound influence of our thoughts and harnessing this knowledge to feel at ease.

The interplay of the Three Principles is omnipresent, shaping every moment of our lives. From the moment we are alive, we have thoughts and become aware of them. This IS the human experience. This is The Human Operating System.

By understanding their interconnected nature and seeing them in action in our daily experiences, we gain profound insights into the nature of our reality and our role within it. It also offers a lens through which to view ourselves and others, recognising the infinite potential and creativity inherent in all of us.

"We don't see things as they are,
we see them as we are."
– Anaïs Nin

Embracing A New Paradigm Of Understanding

The journey through the landscape of the Three Principles, as elucidated by Syd Banks, opens up vistas of insight that challenge many of the conventional frameworks through which we interpret our existence. As you stand on the precipice of this new understanding, it is worth pausing to absorb the magnitude of its implications.

Reflecting on the Profound Impact of the Three Principles on Modern Psychology and Personal Development

Modern psychology has often been a dance between exploring the human condition's external circumstances and probing the inner recesses of the mind. For a significant part of the 20th century, psychology and psychotherapy were heavily influenced by a reductionist model that sought to analyse, diagnose and 'fix' perceived issues within individuals. In fact, modern psychology and psychiatry has been built around the premise of fixing a problem with a solution. Then along came the Three Principles, like a breath of fresh air, suggesting that our experience of life isn't just the product of external events or even our personal histories but is always shaped from the inside-out.

Understanding that Mind, Thought and Consciousness underpin all human experience revolutionises our approach to mental health, relationships, personal development, business success and our understanding of the nature of reality itself.

Realising that our feelings are born from thought and not directly from external circumstances, offers us freedom. The realisation that a vast reservoir of intelligence and potential lies within each of us, waiting to be tapped into, is empowering and enjoyable.

This shift has led to therapeutic practices that focus on awakening individuals to their innate health and resilience, rather than being entrenched in the narratives of their past.

Encouragement for Continued Exploration and Learning

This brief voyage into this understanding is not a destination but a continual journey of discovery. We live and we learn. As we peel back the layers, there are always more insights waiting to be unveiled. Every moment presents an opportunity to deepen our realisation of the Principles and thus with the essence of who we truly are.

Embracing the Principles is not about adopting a new set of beliefs or dogmas, but about fostering a productive relationship with the **foundational truths of our existence.** It's an invitation to be curious, to question our assumptions and attachments and to explore life with a sense of wonder.

To everyone venturing into this profound understanding: remain open, be compassionate with yourself and cherish the insights as they unfold. The Three Principles are not concepts. They are fundamental truths, applicable to all, everywhere.

Like gravity, these Principles are universal: applicable 100% of the time, no exceptions. As we continue to explore, learn and grow, we find that these Principles, though simple, offer a lifetime of depth guiding us towards a richer, more connected and harmonious existence.

In conclusion, as Syd Banks so beautifully expressed, "If the only thing people learned was not to be afraid of their experience, that alone would change the world." Embrace this new paradigm, for in it lies the promise of transformation and peace.

With this introduction to the Three Principles, we hope we have reawakened something in you. Everyone already knows this; we have just forgotten it, with our layers upon layers of innocent misunderstanding and unproductive thinking. In the following pages, we have outlined numerous resources for you to deepen your understanding, many of them from the teachers who pointed us in this direction. We hope you find them as useful as this book.

Recommended Reading And Resources

The journey into the Three Principles and the teachings of Syd Banks is vast, with a plethora of resources available to deepen one's understanding. For those looking to delve further, here's a curated list of reading and resources that provide a comprehensive exploration of these profound insights.

BOOKS:

The Missing Link: Reflections on Philosophy and Spirit by Syd Banks - This seminal work dives deep into the essence of the Three Principles. It's a must-read for anyone looking to understand the foundation of this transformative understanding.

The Enlightened Gardener by Syd Banks - Through a fictional narrative, Banks elucidates the teachings of the Three Principles, offering profound insights in a digestible format.

Second Chance by Syd Banks

The Enlightened Gardener - Revisited' by Syd Banks

Dear Liza by Syd Banks

In Quest of the Pearl by Syd Banks

Invisible Power: Insight Principles at Work by Ken Manning, Robin Charbit, and Sandra Krot - This book explores the application of the Three Principles in a professional context enabling readers to enhance their work lives.

Somebody Should Have Told Us! Simple Truths for Living Well by Jack Pransky - Pransky offers a refreshing look at the transformative power of the Three Principles in everyday life.

Clarity: Clear Mind, Better Performance, Bigger Results by Jamie Smart - Smart delves into how understanding the Principles can lead to clarity, which in turn can enhance performance in various facets of life.

Do Nothing! Stop Looking, Start Living by Damian Mark Smyth. Damian's first book on the Three Principles which also tells his own story and how it has helped him and many others live a happier life.

Coming Home by Dicken Bettinger and Natasha Swerdloff

Our True Identity... Three Principles by Elsie Spittle

Paradigm Shift: A History of The Three Principles by George Pransky, Jack Pransky

Seduced by Consciousness: A Life with The Three Principles by Jack Pransky

The Inside-Out Revolution: The Only Thing You Need to Know to Change Your Life Forever by Michael Neill

The Space Within: Finding Your Way Back Home by Michael Neill

Inside Out Transformation: A Revolutionary Guide for Coaches, Therapists and Counsellors. Conversations with 15 Renowned Leaders by Sheela Masand and Michael Neill

The Little Book of Results: A Quick Guide to Achieving Big Goals by Jamie Smart

REAL: The Inside-Out Guide to Being Yourself by Clare Dimond

The He'art of Thriving: Musings On the Human Experience by Kimberley Hare

A Little Peace of Mind: The Revolutionary Solution for Freedom from Anxiety, Panic Attacks and Stress by Nicola Bird

Just a Thought: A No-Willpower Approach to Overcome Self-Doubt and Make Peace with Your Mind by Amy Johnson

The Little Book of Big Change: The No-Willpower

Approach by Amy Johnson

Instant Motivation: The surprising truth behind what really drives performance by Chantal Burns

Stillpower: The Inner Source of Athletic Excellence by Garret Kramer

The Path of No Resistance: Why Overcoming Is Simpler Than You Think by Garret Kramer

The Relationship Handbook by George S. Pransky

Parenting From the Heart by Jack Pransky

The Spark Inside by Ami Mills Naim

The Speed Trap by Joe Bailey

The Serenity Principle: Finding Peace in Recovery by Joe Bailey

Inside Out Izzy by Angela Mastwijk

What is a Thought? (A thought is a lot) by Jack Pransky and Amy Kahofer

What is Wisdom (and where do I find it)? by Jack Pransky and Amy Kahofer

[There are many other books available now on Amazon about the Three Principles, so this list is not exclusive].

CD'S AND DVD'S
Lectures by Sydney Banks

These four lectures by Sydney Banks are the ones that we recommend to people who are new to the Three Principles and who want to get to grips with the key messages.

Hawaii Lectures by Sydney Banks

This series of four lectures delivered in Oahu in 2001 carries the philosopher's central message: "If you can find the true nature of Mind, Consciousness and Thought, you'll free yourself for the rest of your life."

The Long Beach lectures by Sydney Banks

In this series, Sydney Banks reflects on spiritual and psychological aspects of the Three Principles and their practical applications in everyday life.

The Washington Lectures by Sydney Banks

These lectures, available in CD or DVD format, comprise some of Syd's most accessible and humorous discussions on the role of Thought in everyday life.

One Thought Away by Sydney Banks

This audio recording captures Syd in full flight as he talks to a receptive audience of ex-offenders, urging them to discard negative thoughts and start a new life in positivity… "We are all just one thought away from mental health."

ARTICLES AND PAPERS:

The Evolution of the Three Principles: From Health Realisation to Innate Health - An insightful paper exploring the development and evolution of the Three Principles understanding.

The Nature of Thought: Explorations in Syd Banks' Teachings - An academic article that delves deep into the philosophical implications of the Three Principles.

ONLINE RESOURCES:

Three Principles Foundation Website - A treasure trove of videos, audios, and articles from Syd Banks and other teachers in the field.

One Thought Institute - Offers courses, seminars, and resources for those looking to understand and apply the Principles in their lives.

Three Principles Movies - A platform featuring movies, webinars and interviews centred around the this understanding.

The Inside-Out Revolution Podcast by Michael Neill - Neill, a well-known figure in the Three Principles community, delves into various topics related to the Principles, featuring interviews with experts and transformative stories.

Devilinagoodman.com/post/2019/03/06/130-sydney-banks-quotes - 130 of Syd Bank's quotes.

These resources offer just a glimpse into the expansive world of the Three Principles. As with any profound understanding, the journey is personal and unique to each individual. Take these recommendations as starting points and let your curiosity guide you deeper into the heart of these transformative teachings.

"Thought is not reality;
yet it is through Thought that
our realities are created."
– Sydney Banks

Human-iOS - Who Are We?

At Human-iOS, we have decades of experience in bringing the understanding of how the human mind actually works into all areas of business, education, therapeutic intervention and more, as well as creating books and podcasts to share with the world. Here is a brief introduction to each of the founding members and contributors to this book in their own words:

Damian Mark Smyth

I came across the Three Principles in 2012 at a conference in London on sales. The event was discussing connection and the host talked about a man named Sydney Banks and how thought created our world and how we were the ones responsible for our own feelings. Although I didn't really understand what the presenter was talking about, something he said was making sense and gave me a feeling of curiosity to learn more.

After this event, I decided to investigate the source of

the content that had made me so curious and bought some books by Mr Banks.

I started with 'The Enlightened Gardner' and although it made sense on an intellectual level, I was struggling to see how it could help me to deal with my depression, OCD (Obsessive Compulsive Disorder) and occasional suicidal thoughts. But as I continued to digest Syd's materials, I started to feel better. It was as though the fog was starting to lift. I didn't know why, but I started to be happier without anything else in my life changing.

As a result of these nice feelings, I continued to explore the Principles and the teachers and mentors who were using this understanding in their work. I attended a Three Principles training by Jack Pransky at the Tikun centre of Jewish learning in London and it was at this event that I started to see glimpses of why I was feeling happier and worrying less, without my life on the 'outside', changing in any way.

Jack talked about Innate Health and how we are all

perfect as we are but for our thinking that we are not. It made so much sense to me, and I remember coming away from those two days thinking that my journey with this understanding was just beginning and I would also be sharing my story with others in the future.

Subsequently, at another event (not Principles related) I learned that writing a book was a great way to get connections within whatever industry sector you wished to be a part of, so I decided to write one on the Three Principles. Little did I know that I would be the first person in the UK to ever release a book on the Principles.

It was during the process of writing 'Do Nothing! - Stop Looking, Start Living' that my understanding deepened - as I was interviewing those who were sharing the Principles, as well as having to tell others about how I saw them myself. There is no better way to learn something than having to explain it simply to others.

My first experience of how powerful knowing that we are innately healthy and that our experience is created by us from the inside out, came when I was asked to help someone who had extreme agoraphobia and depression.

During our brief conversation, I only shared how we all see things differently and how we use the same process to create different results (separate realities). The person with whom I spoke had a severe diagnosis, having been in therapy for 28 years after suffering abuse as a child. I can't remember exactly what was said, but as a result of our discussion, I learned later that this lady had gone from being a recluse of 20 years to going on safari in Africa, forgiving her perpetrators completely and rejoining life completely as a mentally healthy individual.

Apparently she realised she had always been healthy but had been creating her own mental torment for decades and was doing it to herself. Powerful!

That was the moment I decided that I needed to

be working with this understanding on a full time basis and became a life-coach/counsellor in the Three Principles.

Over the years, my niche became entrepreneurs and business owners who were stuck in their thinking. As I worked with them to show how their minds were operating, they became lighter and more connected and started to solve their own issues with ease.

I created and ran a course called 'The Will to Act' for The Entrepreneurs Circle, which to this day still has former attendees coming up to me at events thanking me for the profound impact it had on their lives and business.

My second book: 'The Entrepreneur Success Formula' outlined how this thinking works and how, as business owners, we get stuck in the misunderstanding of how our minds operate.

Subsequently, I have delivered three TEDx talks (all available on YouTube) on Purpose, Entrepreneurial

Thinking and Understanding the Mind to Solve Problems.

I have created podcasts talking about the Principles and written hundreds of blog articles on how our minds operate and what it means for humanity to know this.

From challenging individuals with extreme diagnoses to complex business issues for large corporations, I have been able to share how our minds operate and point people back to their innate wisdom to solve issues for themselves.

damian.smyth@human-ios.consulting

Flavia Dalzell Payne

I was painfully shy as a child. As I grew up, however, I was surrounded by supportive family and friends and it appeared to all that I sailed through life. But I was moody, and deep down I lacked self-belief and harboured feelings of inadequacy.

Because of this lack of self-confidence, I was a chameleon moulding myself to fit in with others. Thriving at times, yet at other times, for reasons I didn't understand, I found myself struggling with debilitating feelings of self-doubt.

Looking back, I can see from the life choices that I made how my behaviour reflected my lack of self-belief. Who was I to aspire to great things? Indeed, who was I?

I played small. I managed to do well in business but suffered from imposter syndrome and never pushed myself.

In a stroke of synchronicity, I ended up working for a Los Angeles-based company called Senn Delaney Leadership who were setting up a London office. Employees were given a CD series to listen to called 'The Foundations of Mental Well-being' by Dr George Pransky, a 3P psychologist and a pioneer in bringing this understanding into the field of psychology. I was also given an entire box of cassettes by a man called Sydney Banks.

I listened. I tried. Several times. Syd talked about how we all lived in a 'world of thought'. I didn't understand a word; it went straight over my head. I grasped a bit more of what George was saying, but not much. So I put the CDs and cassettes away and forgot about them for almost 20 years.

Forward wind those years, I find myself divorced in my mid-40s and training to become a Mindset Coach. As I studied the curriculum and learned about the power of our thoughts to realise our dreams, I felt that something was missing and that there was more to learn about thought.

One day, during this time of reflection, I rediscovered Dr Pransky's CD series hidden away in the back of a cupboard. The only place I had a CD player was in the car, so one morning having dropped my children off at school, I put the CD into the car stereo. George's calm voice came over the airwaves. As I listened, totally enthralled at hearing his voice again after all these years, I got goosebumps. "This is it," I thought, "this is the missing piece I have been looking for! It's seeing how our thinking creates our experience of life and understanding the innate health and resilience of the human mind." **This is the secret to mental health**, I realised. I felt thrilled and daunted all at the same time.

For the next 7 years I threw myself headlong into learning about the Principles from the first-generation teachers (those who were mentored directly by Syd Banks), including being personally mentored by both George and Linda Pransky. I have learned so much from them.

Initially though, I merged what little I understood

about the Principles with the Mindset Coaching, working with individuals and groups, schools (Sixth Formers) and at-risk youth and young offenders, but, as time passed, I realised more and more the truth and simplicity of the Principles and began to see that they were the only route to go. I dropped everything else.

My first client had a complete life shift from learning this understanding. She had a close friend who was a Metropolitan Police Officer, and word spread. One day my client's friend called asking if I would be willing to be the keynote speaker to 250 police officers at a Met Well-being event. I was thrilled and daunted again, but I had learned enough by now not to take my thoughts of self-doubt seriously and I was able to look to more helpful and productive thinking. I was delighted to accept the invitation.

On the day of the talk, I felt calm, confident and honoured to be on stage talking about the resilience of the human potential with that particular group of people who can benefit so much from this understanding, considering the daily crises and challenges they face.

They resonated deeply with what I was able to share.

This understanding has not only transformed my life, but has set me on the path to realising my full potential.

Having spent my professional life in the business world, I always intuited that I would one day return to that sphere to share this understanding, and, through meeting Damian and Tim, I am delighted to be a part of Human-iOS Consulting. I look forward to sharing this simple, yet profound and life-changing understanding with as many people as possible.

flavia.dp@human-ios.consulting

Tim Gunner

As a qualified psychotherapist, I am a lifelong learner. Learning the Three Principles and understanding their implications is probably the most important knowledge I have discovered and taught to date.

These Principles have far-reaching implications for everyone, affecting school, teenage years, relationships, family life, business, mental health, absenteeism, addictive behaviour, confidence, worry and anxiety. To say that this is life-changing and has contributed to saving lives is no overestimation. I know this to be true.

In 2008, I returned to academia once again, embarking on a course of study in Hypnotherapy at college while integrating Psychoanalysis, Brief Solution Therapy, NLP (Neuro-Linguistic Programming) and CBT (Cognitive Behavioural Therapy). During a lunch break with colleagues, a chance conversation with a fellow participant who mentioned Sydney Banks, led me to discover the Three Principles for myself.

That night in 2008, I went back to Google what I could. I heard something truthful and deeply useful in what I found. It was simple, yet I doubted that anything that good could be that simple. After a lifetime of learning skills, tools, techniques, 'how to's,' and strategies that work, I thought there must be more to it. I already had a deep understanding of human behaviour, behavioural change and psychology. Was there really something that I and everyone else had missed? The answer is yes.

My friend took me to a meeting in Birmingham where everyone looked suspiciously happy. The facilitator, Janet, talked about how she had got caught up in thought about her relationship and the effect that had on her experience of it that day, in the moment. I could see how this worked in my life and also how, in a moment of insight, that could change totally.

At the time, I was a Senior Practitioner in a voluntary sector addiction, drugs and alcohol organisation, and a psychotherapist within the NHS at a busy Birmingham GP practice, with ten years of service in mental health services already under my belt. I knew Janet Rhynie from the busiest probation office in the country where she was working at the time. I came to see how useful this learning is in the field of mental health, communities, addiction and criminal justice and was introduced to the work of Dr. Roger Mills, Jack Pransky, Dr. Bill Pettit and Dr. George Pransky. I also started seeing the implications in my own life. Something began to shift.

That year and the next, a colleague and I were recipients of National Training Awards for our training and support programs delivered. I decided to leave work to join a management development consultancy as a partner.

The Bridge is an international consulting group offering organisations a new way to look at culture change, organisation and leadership development and coaching. At The Bridge, I worked for 14 years with some of the world's most admired global organisations, integrating this learning alongside training workshops and long-term programs in leadership, innovation, communication, cross-cultural effectiveness, teamwork and coaching for business.

I wanted to learn more, so I attended a couple of introductory courses run by some people who learned directly from Sydney Banks, Rudy and Jenny (now Elleray) Kennard. They were the creators of Three Principles Movies, a site dedicated to sharing the Principles as first articulated by the late Sydney Banks, which was a useful place to find content. Again, the room was full of people who looked suspiciously happy and some of them talked about love, peace, and other things I thought were a bit esoteric, but I gained even more awareness and understanding.

The messages were simple, but I was looking for something deeper. I had a business background in retail, distribution and marketing and a very logical psychoanalytical brain. I took my wife along too; she thought it was amazing and took a lot from it. It helped our relationship and offered us a shared understanding of each other, the world and other people.

I enlisted a coach, read lots of books and attended a few conferences at the Tikun centre of Jewish learning in London and elsewhere. I trained with Michael Neill and Jamie Smart, two people in the world of the Principles who made sense and resonated with me due to bringing something new to the table. I also knew them previously through the world of NLP. Their articulation was about innate health and well-being through subtractive psychology. The idea that this understanding literally 'takes things off your mind' and how tricky, sticky and also how much fun reality can be.

I participated in one of Jamie Smart's first year-long programs and gained a great deal of clarity of understanding and articulation under his mentoring and tutorship. His book 'Clarity – Clear Mind, Better Performance, Bigger Results' is still one of the best I have ever read.

The first book on the Principles I read was actually my colleague Damian's book 'Do Nothing! Stop Looking, Start Living,' which really spelled out the misunderstanding of our individual thought systems and how that causes our problems and all other problems, pain and suffering in the world. I saw how reactive thinking blocks our natural flow of intelligence and creativity. It made it clear that the trick is simply to see how the trick is done. That's it, no more.

Countless books, webinars, trainings and workshops later, wondering what to do next led me back into working with young people and parents. I have had, what could be termed, a colourful youth. A story I am happy to share throughout my life as a result, so I have always been involved with youth and community.

I knew Terry Rubenstein from Tikun and was mentored by her and the wider team at the worldwide charity she founded, called iHeart (Innate Health Education and Resilience Training), in London. With iHeart, I simplified and honed my understanding of the nature of our psychological system and how our well-being gets covered up.

I now share this with teenagers and parents online,

face to face, in schools and other settings. Many young people have been impacted regarding suicidal ideation, self-harm, autism, ADHD, eating disorders and addictions via my tutoring at iHeart. I am grateful to have played my part in delivery and fundraising at this vital charity attempting to go upstream to address the teenage mental health crisis we currently face.

Damian and I share many hobbies and interests, so we became good friends when we met around 2018. We talked about working together, founded Human-iOS and started running webinars on the Three Principles during the pandemic. I met Flavia in 2023 and I am happy to be part of the team.

tim.gunner@human-ios.consulting

Visit www.human-ios.consulting to learn more about how we can help you and your business to tap into your team's potential and improve performance and productivity by understanding The Human Operating System.

Space For Insights

As your understanding of the Principles deepens, you will no doubt see things differently. We have found that having space to keep notes of emerging insights can be very useful on your journey.